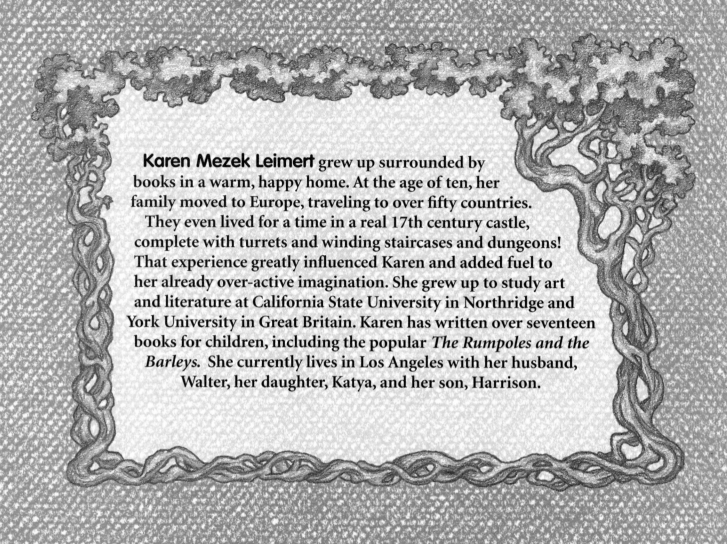

Karen Mezek Leimert grew up surrounded by books in a warm, happy home. At the age of ten, her family moved to Europe, traveling to over fifty countries. They even lived for a time in a real 17th century castle, complete with turrets and winding staircases and dungeons! That experience greatly influenced Karen and added fuel to her already over-active imagination. She grew up to study art and literature at California State University in Northridge and York University in Great Britain. Karen has written over seventeen books for children, including the popular *The Rumpoles and the Barleys.* She currently lives in Los Angeles with her husband, Walter, her daughter, Katya, and her son, Harrison.

GOODNIGHT BLESSINGS

by
Karen Mezek Leimert

NELSON

Thomas Nelson, Inc.
Nashville

Goodnight Blessings

MANAGING EDITOR: *Laura Minchew*
PROJECT EDITOR: *Brenda Ward*

Library of Congress Cataloging-in-Publication Data

Leimert, Karen Mezek, 1956–
  Goodnight blessings/by Karen Mezek Leimert.
   p. cm.
  ISBN 0–8499–1134–6 (hardcover)
  ISBN 0–8499–5808–3 (tradepaper)
1. Children—Prayer-books and devotions—English. 2. God—Worship and love—Juvenile literature. [1. Prayer books and devotions.]
I. Title.
BV265.L45 1994

242'.62—dc20

93–41583
CIP
AC

Printed in the United States of America

97 98 99 00 01 LBM 9 8 7 6 5 4 3 2 1

For my mom

God bless you now and always.

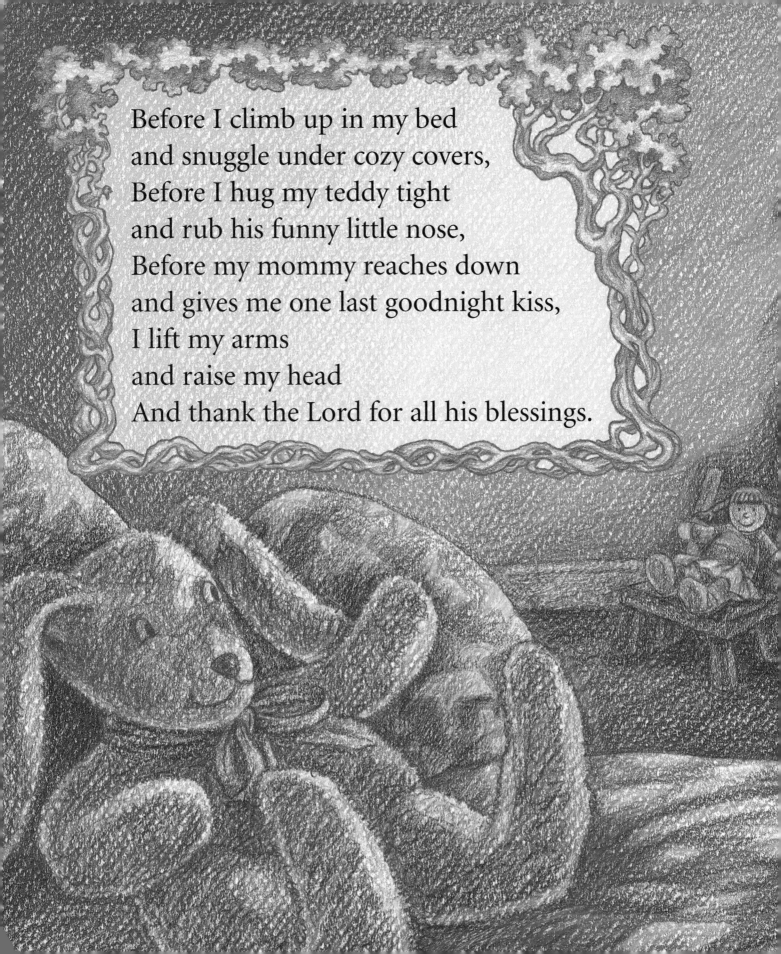

Before I climb up in my bed
and snuggle under cozy covers,
Before I hug my teddy tight
and rub his funny little nose,
Before my mommy reaches down
and gives me one last goodnight kiss,
I lift my arms
and raise my head
And thank the Lord for all his blessings.

Thank you for sweet smelling flowers,
faces lifted to the . . .

SKY

Thank you for the cloudy sky,
filled with drippy drops of . . .

Thank you for the splashing rain,
falling down on rocky . . .

PEAKS

Thank you for the snowy peaks,
rising up above the . . .

EARTH

Thank you for the rich, green earth,
home to stomping, roaring . . .

BEASTS

Thank you for the furry beasts,
loved by me and all God's . . .

CHILDREN

Thank you for your busy children;
one of them is my best . . .

Thank you for my favorite friend;
we play all day beside the . . .

SEA

Thank you for the shimmering sea,
filled with shiny, swimming . . .

FISH

Thank you for the glittery fish;
I watch them with my . . .

MOM and DAD

Thank you for my mom and dad;
they read to me beneath the . . .

MOON

Thank you for the glowing moon,
reaching down and giving me . . .

one last goodnight kiss.

Goodnight.